贝贝熊系列丛书
The Berenstain Bears

AF697293

and the GREEN-EYED MONSTER

甩开嫉妒心

第一时间的启蒙书

贝贝熊系列丛书

The Berenstain Bears

AND THE GREEN-EYED MONSTER

甩开嫉妒心

（美）斯坦·博丹　简·博丹　绘著

Stan & Jan Berenstain

孙志芳等　译

新疆青少年出版社

大树屋门前有一条金色的土路，通往熊王国的深处，此时，树屋里满是欢声笑语——有人过生日啦！

过生日的是小熊哥哥，今天，他会收到许多精美的礼物。起初，他并没有打算举办一个生日派对，但是弗雷德表兄、丽兹和巴伯布鲁诺都来了。当然，爷爷和奶奶也来了。

“哇哦！”小熊哥哥打开爷爷送的礼物，是一支棒球棍！

“谢谢爷爷，有了它我肯定能打出二十个全垒打！”

奶奶的礼物是一件夹克衫，穿上去帅气又暖和。小熊哥哥穿着它，对着镜子照个不停。

“谢谢奶奶，太棒了！”

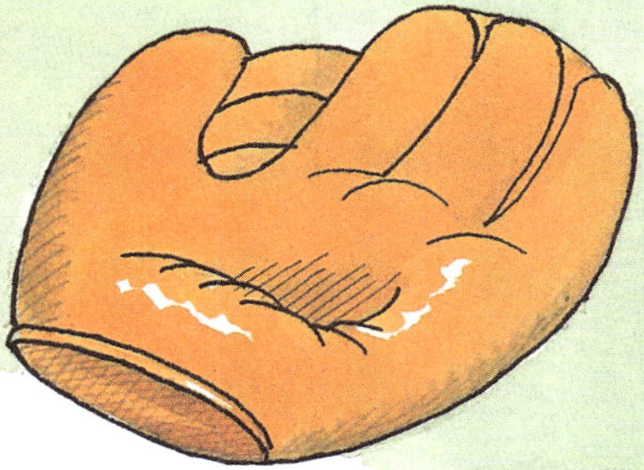

小熊哥哥的生日礼物还有弗雷德表兄送的棒球手套、丽兹送的体育影碟和巴伯布鲁诺送的探险小说。小熊妹妹的贴心礼物是一包特制木板,是特意为小熊哥哥组装飞机模型准备的。

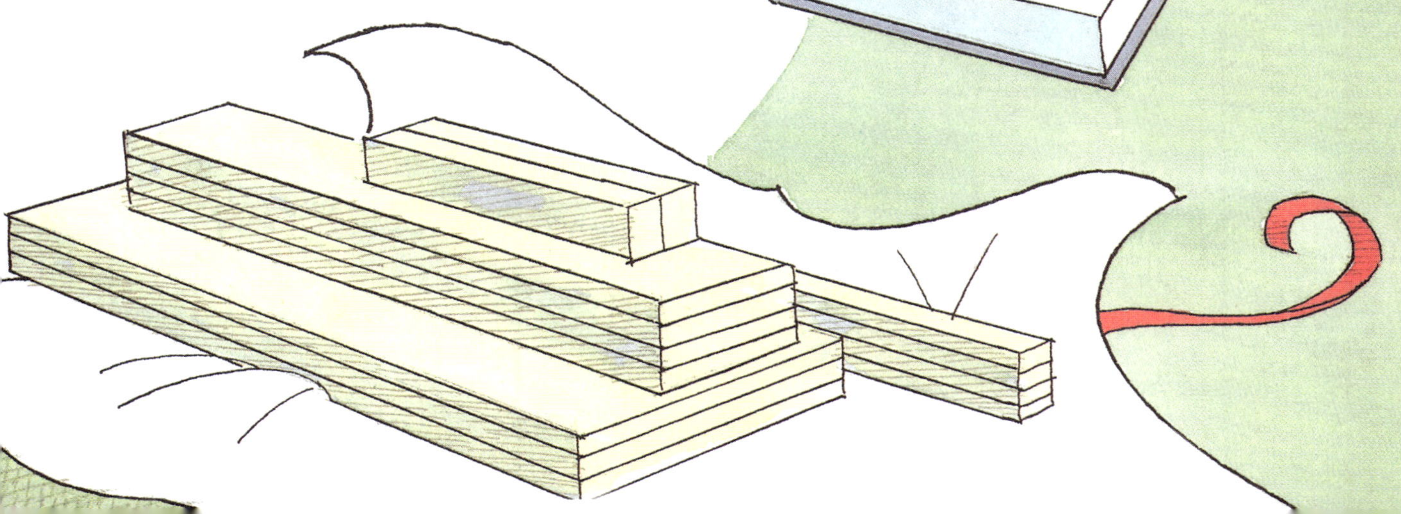

"谢谢！谢谢！谢谢大家！"小熊哥哥激动地说。
"不客气，祝你生日快乐！"大家异口同声地说。

小熊妹妹的礼物是精心准备的，但她现在正想着另一件事——哥哥一下子收到那么多的礼物，自己却没有，她感到忿忿不平。小熊妹妹试着安慰自己：在她过生日的时候也收到过很多礼物，下次生日的时候还会收到。再说，反正她对棒球棍啊、夹克衫啊、棒球手套啊、体育影碟啊，还有木头什么的一点儿也不感兴趣。

而当熊爸爸和熊妈妈亮出他们的礼物时，小熊妹妹再也没法安慰自己了。那是一辆小熊妹妹见过的，最大、最漂亮的变速越野自行车。那辆车有线儿闸，有三档变速，还有运动型轮胎。小熊妹妹看见这么漂亮的自行车，脑子里想的不再是“哥哥，生日快乐”，而是“我也想要那辆车！我要！我要！！我要!!!”。

祝小熊哥哥：
生日快乐

熊妈妈注意到小熊妹妹一脸“我也想要”的表情，她把小熊妹妹带到一边，帮她回忆上次小熊妹妹过生日时收到的许多精美的礼物。可小熊妹妹一个字也听不进去，她只是两眼直勾勾地盯着那辆有线儿闸、三档变速和运动型轮胎的，又大又漂亮的越野自行车。“哦，宝贝儿，”熊妈妈说，“我想你大概是被‘绿眼妖怪’缠上了。”

“‘绿眼妖怪’？”小熊妹妹问道，“那是什么？”

“哦，”熊妈妈解释说，“那只是一种用来形容妒忌的说法。你知道妒忌是什么了，妒忌就是，你很想得到属于别人的东西。”

“但是，妈妈，”小熊妹妹说，“那辆车实在太棒了，太漂亮了！”

“宝贝儿，听我说，”熊妈妈说，“就算你有了那样的车，你也没法儿骑，你还太小，连脚踏板都够不着。再说，快看，爸爸给你拿什么来了？”熊爸爸推着小熊哥哥的儿童自行车走了过来，车后还加上了帮助保持平衡的小轮子。

“现在它是你的了。”熊爸爸说。小熊妹妹看着哥哥淘汰下来的车，它也不错，但它没有线儿闸，不能三档变速，也没有运动型轮胎。

“过来，孩子们，”熊妈妈说，“我们的客人要走了，该说‘再见’了。”

“再见！”小熊哥哥说，“谢谢你们大家的生日礼物！”

“再见。”小熊妹妹说。爷爷和奶奶上了他们的卡车，回家去了。

丽兹和其他人上了她爸爸的汽车，布鲁因先生答应送他们回家。

熊爸爸帮小熊哥哥把新自行车搬下楼梯，熊妈妈和熊爸爸骄傲地看着小熊哥哥骑上车，试了起来。

起初，小熊哥哥只是骑着车绕着树屋飞快地转圈，后来又做了几个前轮离地的特技，当他干脆把脚放在了车把上时，熊妈妈开始担心了。

“别太冒失了！”她大声提醒说。

小熊妹妹也看着呢。她走进屋里，一动不动地盯着窗外。看着看着，妒忌心越来越膨胀，从她的粉色发带一直蔓延到她的脚趾尖上。小熊妹妹实在太想要那辆又大、又漂亮的越野自行车了。

晚上，小熊妹妹还在想着那辆自行车，怎么也睡不着。就在她终于快要睡着的时候，奇怪的事情发生了：小熊妹妹家来了一位客人，这位客人长得和小熊妹妹一模一样，除了她的绿眼睛和头上的小犄角。“我知道你是谁，”小熊妹妹说，“你就是‘绿眼妖怪’。”

当然，小熊妹妹只是在做梦，但她并没有意识到这是梦，它是那么真实。

“来，”“绿眼妖怪”说，“只要你能证明自己可以骑，你就能得到一辆哥哥那样的自行车。”

小熊妹妹还没弄明白是怎么回事，就已经坐上了车，“绿眼妖怪”在她背后狠狠地推了一把。

这辆车对小熊妹妹来说真是太大了，她甚至连脚踏板也够不着。接下来，就像所有梦境一样，事情开始变得荒诞起来。自行车越来越大，越来越大！

这时，自行车已经无法控制，加速冲下山去。山脚下有一块大岩石，她不偏不倚地撞了上去，撞得太厉害了！小熊哥哥崭新的生日礼物被摔得粉碎。“我都做了些什么呀！”小熊妹妹尖叫着，“我都做了些什么呀！”

熊妈妈和熊爸爸刚刚睡着，听到声音马上冲到孩子们的床前。“哦，妈妈！”小熊妹妹哭着说，“我刚刚把哥哥那辆漂亮的越野自行车撞成了碎片！全撞碎了！”

“来，冷静点儿，宝贝儿，”熊妈妈说，“小熊哥哥的车好好的，什么事儿都没有，你刚才是在做梦。”

“怎么了？”小熊哥哥揉着眼睛问。

“我下楼去给大家拿点儿热牛奶来，”熊爸爸说，“它能帮我们睡个好觉。”

的确如此。

第二天，小熊妹妹最好的朋友丽兹来找她玩儿。她和小熊妹妹骑着车，围着院子跑来跑去，玩得可高兴了。小熊妹妹骑着小熊哥哥的那辆旧车很顺手，丽兹骑着小熊妹妹的那辆旧车也很开心。小熊哥哥骑着自己漂亮的越野自行车绕着她们转。

不久，当布鲁因先生来接丽兹时，他给大家带来了一个大惊喜——他刚刚用自己那辆旧车换回了一辆全新的汽车：橡胶轮胎、真皮座椅以及跑车外形，多棒的一辆车啊！

熊妈妈、小熊兄妹和丽兹都祝贺布鲁因先生有了新车，除了熊爸爸以外。他只是站在那里，看着。和小熊妹妹当初看见哥哥的新自行车时一样，熊爸爸也是一脸“我也想要”的表情。

“爸爸，”小熊妹妹说，“我觉得你最好提防……你知道是谁！”

熊爸爸当然知道是谁。

“布鲁因先生，”他上前握住布鲁因先生的手说，“祝贺你有了一辆漂亮的新车！”

布鲁因父女离开后，熊妈妈和熊爸爸坐在树屋的台阶上，看着小熊哥哥和小熊妹妹骑在各自的自行车上，玩得十分开心。

The Berenstain Bears and the GREEN-EYED MONSTER

When another bear gets something brand new,
the Green-eyed Monster makes <u>you</u> want one, too.

1. It was a happy time in the big tree house down a sunny dirt road in Bear Country—a happy birthday time.

It was Brother Bear's birthday, and he was getting some very fine presents. Brother wasn't exactly having a party, but Cousin Fred, Lizzy Bruin, and Babs Bruno were there. And Gramps and Gran, of course.

2. "Wow!" said Brother when he opened his present from Gramps. It was an aluminum bat.

"Thanks, Gramps. I'll hit twenty home runs with this!"

Gran's present was a great-looking warm-up jacket. Brother tried it on and looked in the mirror.

"Thank you, Gran. It's really neat," he said.

His other presents were a fielder's glove from Cousin Fred, a sports video from Lizzy Bruin, and a mystery book from Babs Bruno. Sister's very thoughtful gift was a package of balsa wood, the special wood Brother used for making model airplanes.

3. "Thank you! Thank you! Thank you all!" he said.

"You're welcome and happy birthday!" said the gift givers.

Sister's gift *was* thoughtful. But she was being thoughtful in another way, too. It isn't always easy when your brother gets a lot of presents and you don't. Sister understood that she had gotten presents when it was her birthday and would again. Besides, she wasn't that interested in aluminum bats, warm-up jackets, fielder's gloves, sports videos, or balsa wood, anyway.

4. But all that changed when Mama and Papa Bear gave Brother *their* present. It was the biggest, most beautiful racing bike Sister had ever seen. It had a hand brake, three speeds, and super-sport wheels. When Sister saw that beautiful bike, it was no longer, “Happy birthday, Brother!” It was, “I gotta have that bike! I gotta! I gotta! I gotta!”

5. Mama saw that I-gotta-have-it look in Sister’s eyes. She took her aside and reminded her about all the wonderful presents she had gotten on her last birthday. *But Sister didn’t hear a word Mama said.* She just stared at that big, beautiful bike with the hand brake and the super-sport wheels. “Oh, dear,” said Mama. “I think you’ve been taken over by the green-eyed monster.”

“Green-eyed monster?” said Sister. “What’s that?”

“Oh,” said Mama. “That’s just a way folks have of talking about jealousy and envy. You know what it means to be jealous. Envy is when you want something that belongs to somebody else.”

“But, Mama,” said Sister. “It’s such a great beautiful bike!”

6. “Please listen to me, Sister,” said Mama. “Even if you had a bike like that, you couldn’t ride it. You’re not big enough. Your feet wouldn’t reach the pedals. Besides, look what Papa’s got for you.” Papa was wheeling in Brother’s junior-size bike with its training wheels attached.

“It’s yours now,” he said. Sister looked at the bike Brother had outgrown. It was okay, but it didn’t have a hand brake, three speeds, and super-sport wheels.

7. “Come on now,” said Mama. “Our guests are leaving. It’s time to say good-bye.”

“Good-bye!” said Brother. “Thank you all for the wonderful presents!”

“Bye,” said Sister. Gramps and Gran got into their pickup truck and headed for home. Lizzy Bruin got into her dad’s car with the others. Mr. Bruin had agreed to come for them and drive them home. Then Papa helped carry the new bike down the front steps. Mama and Papa watched proudly as Brother climbed on and tried it out.

8. First Brother rode big, fast circles around the tree house. Then he did a few wheelies. When he started riding with his feet up on the handlebars, Mama got worried.

"Now let's not be reckless!" she said.

Sister watched, too. She had gone inside and was watching from a window. As she did so she became filled with envy. From the tips of her pink hairbow down to the tips of her toenails, *Sister really wanted that big, beautiful racing bike.*

9. That night Sister was having trouble falling asleep because she was still thinking about the bike. Then just as her eyes were closing the strangest thing happened. She had a visitor. The visitor looked exactly like Sister, except she was green and had little horns on her head. "I know who you are," Sister said. "You're the green-eyed monster."

10. Sister was having a dream, of course. But she didn't know that. That's the thing about dreams. They're so *real.*

"Come," said the green-eyed monster. "If you want a bike like Brother's, all you have to do is prove you're big enough to ride it."

Before she quite knew what was happening, she was up on the bike and the green-eyed monster was giving her a big push.

11. The bike was much too big for her. Her feet couldn't even *almost* reach the pedals. Then, as so often happens in dreams, things began to change. The bike got bigger and *bigger* and BIGGER!

Now Sister was speeding down a hill. At the bottom was a great rock. She smashed into it. There was a huge crash! Brother's beautiful new birthday bike flew into a thousand pieces. "What have I done?" she screamed. "What have I done?"

12. Mama and Papa, who had just fallen asleep, came running into the cubs' room. "Oh, Mama!" cried Sister. "I just smashed Brother's beautiful birthday bike into a thousand pieces! A thousand pieces!"

"Try to calm down, sweetie," said Mama. "Brother's bike is perfectly safe. You were having a dream."

"What's going on?" said Brother, rubbing his eyes.

"I'll go downstairs and get us all some warm milk," said Papa. "It'll help us get back to sleep."

And it did.

13. The next day Sister's best friend, Lizzy, came over to play. She and Sister had a fun time riding around the yard. Brother's old bike turned out to be just right for Sister. Lizzy had a good time on Sister's old trike. And Brother rode circles around them on his birthday bike.

Later, when Mr. Bruin came over to pick up Lizzy, he had a very big surprise for everybody. He had just traded in his old car for a beautiful brand-new one. And what a car it was! It had wire wheels, leather seats, and racing stripes.

14. Mama, Brother, Sister, and Lizzy congratulated Mr. Bruin on his fine new car. But not Papa. He just stood and stared. He had the same I-gotta-have-it look that Sister had when she first saw Brother's new bike.

"Papa," said Sister. "I think you better watch out for 'you know who'!"

Papa did know who.

"Mr. Bruin," he said, "congratulations on a fine new car!"

15. After the Bruins drove away, Mama and Papa sat on the tree house steps and watched Brother and Sister do some plain and fancy bike riding.